For: J

From: E

Thank you for being such
an inspiration to me!

GRACE OVER DRAMA

(A DEFINITION OF GOD)

by

Patricia Van Riper

the Peppertree Press, LLC
Sarasota, Florida

HIGH HOPES

Next time you're found,
with your chin on the ground

There's a lot to be learned
so look around

Sarah Jane and Patty Ann —Taken 3/10/45

DEDICATED TO:

Sarah Jane

My mother and inspiration
For her "high-in-the-sky apple pie" hopes!

Kenneth

My loving husband
Champion for the "underdog"
(four-legged and two)

Friends of Bill W

"Our stories disclose in a general way what we used
to be like, what happened, and what we are like now.
If you have decided you want what we have and are
willing to go to any length to get it—then you are
ready to take certain steps."

Special Moments Captured Between Sarah Jane And Ken

INTRODUCTION

After extensive testing, my mother Sarah Jane is diagnosed with Alzheimer's disease just prior to her 65th birthday. The remaining twelve years of her life are challenging for both family and close friends.

The expression, "It's not about the destination; it's about the journey," takes on new meaning. Following the path of this debilitating illness, we travel from "nowhere" to "now here" to "now what." As her only child, I sought out the guidance of professionals and support groups.

A long the way, I realized that my mother's grief was just as raw and real as mine. I watched as she shed layers of clothing (often literally). Any knowledge of current events, short-term memories, perspective of day from night, socializing, food choices, entertainment, and even the freedom to travel from place to place without supervision or a "designated driver" were taken away.

What tools could I use to bring me into her world and how could I accept the unacceptable and fill the void left for both of us? I began to communicate with her by letting her take me where her memories were. I might be her daughter one day and a stranger the next and yet, she is still here. She taught me how to live "in the now" and just "be."

I released my mother and myself from the need to be perfect. We watched comedy: silly, bawdy and ridiculous episodes of Laurel and Hardy, The Three Stooges, and Benny Hill. We found them to be brilliant beacons of hope and oh, how we laughed.

My mother lived with the disease of Alzheimer's, just as I live with the disease of Alcoholism. An affirmation that I use daily is, "I am going to forgive myself for needing to be forgiven."

"If you want what we have and are willing to go to any length to get it." The social worker on the floor provides me with a meeting schedule as I am discharged from the psych floor of a local hospital. By the age of 38, alcoholism lays claim to my physical, emotional, and spiritual wellbeing, leaving behind a "drama queen" with the maturity of an adolescent at best.

My first meeting is held in a smoke-filled church basement, and it is here that I learn that I never have to be alone again. During that hour, strangers share their experience, strength, and hope. The unconditional love offered to me sustains me enough to believe that, just for today, I can recover from a seemingly hopeless, helpless state of mind and body.

My mother's illness and mine are two diseases for which

there is no known medical cure. While my mother died over twenty years ago, I continue to have a daily reprieve, if I do not pick up that first drink.

While Alzheimer's disease took her cognitive ability, my mother remained a woman of grace and dignity. As my mother became less and less available to her loved ones, she became more and more available to the God of her understanding, and it is here that she found the peace and acceptance that radiated to others.

Mom, Dad And Me
Stolp Avenue, Syracuse, NY

Table of Contents

AMAZING GRACE

Aunt Sarah, Mom, Dad and Aunts

Someone to Watch over Me

My parents' love story begins when a tall, handsome gentleman enters the bank. Waiting his turn in the teller line, a shapely brunette with soft brown eyes catches his attention. Composed and confident, she has no idea how much her life is about to change. Chemistry and fate propel them forward when this gal with a "sweep you off your feet" smile meets this "knock your socks off" guy. Uncharacteristically, she cancels a long-standing date and one year later, they are married in the Catholic Church she attends. Wedding photos speak of a grand couple who could easily step off the cover of *Vogue* magazine and into blissful married life. The defeat and melancholy expressed in later photos tell a different story.

The church bells ring and the neighbor's dog barks incessantly. My mother and I are walking to the Sunday morning service, when she announces that she has a surprise waiting for me after church. Annie, my mother's friend and downstairs neighbor, is waiting for me and together we head to the corner soda fountain while my mother returns home. Seated at the counter on round metal stools, we study the menu. I order my signature tuna salad sandwich served on Wonder bread, with a chocolate malted milkshake as a chaser. Before long, the all-too-familiar voice inside my head speaks to me, "Go home now."

Already an accomplished worrier at the age of seven, I suddenly experience what I can only describe as an impending sense of doom. I will come to recognize this later as my first panic attack. Is my mother safe? Should I be there to protect her? The bread sticks to the roof of my mouth. The half-finished milkshake has lost all appeal.

With my stomach in knots, our trek home feels more like a death march. The stairs leading to the second floor are steep and covered with worn carpeting. Pausing on the landing, I listen for my father's voice.

My mother leads me into our small living room. The curtains and blinds are open, allowing a soft breeze to dispel the powerful force that has been shrinking our family with its rage.

I learn that my father has been removed from our home and taken to a facility where he can receive treatment for the puzzling illness that changes him from Dr. Jekyll into Mr. Hyde.

An image of my father materializes before my eyes. Slumped over on the sofa, staring off into the space of his own twilight zone with a whiskey bottle in one hand, and reaching for a murky glass with the other.

My father, a sensitive, gentle, and soft-spoken man transitions into an angry and demanding taskmaster, summoning my mother for another beer, while hurling the empty bottle at her retreating back. Without her charming prince, my mother and I are forced to face a future without him, as he wobbles under the staggering blow of alcoholism.

Riding the Bus with Sarah Jane

Our bus ride on an early Saturday morning follows James Street with its mansions and richly landscaped properties. The day spreads out before us like a quilt of many colors.

Entering the sanctuary of the public library and following my mother's instructions, I speak softly and use my "inside" voice. Books, colorful flyers, and wire racks filled with pamphlets and bookmarks cover a long mahogany desk, where a perky-voiced lady helps a patron. Suddenly the telephone rings, jarring this hushed environment.

What a treasure house! With so many choices, I can barely contain my excitement as a prince and princess jump off the cover of one book and a pokey puppy beckons to me from another. On our bus ride home, my mother begins to read to me, and my imagination takes flight.

Peter Pan and Tinker Bell sprinkle fairy dust on my pillow, while Puss in Boots, Jack and the Beanstalk, and Alice in Wonderland weave their way into my dreams as my mother nurses me back to health until my fever breaks.

Covered with an angry red rash, measles, (a rapacious predator) invades my body and eventually infects my sore eyes as well. After consulting with my doctor and returning downtown, I'm fitted with my first pair of glasses—thick flesh-color frames and coke-bottle lenses that cover almost half my face.

My mother's smile, with tears in her beautiful brown eyes, greets me as I study my reflection in the window on our bus ride home. I will never forget those excursions and how precious they are to me now that she is no longer with me. The stories, like her unconditional love, remain imbedded in my heart and mind forever.

Abbandanza and Away We Go

A swinging door leads to the kitchen, where a swarm of worker bees assemble a large antipasto salad concocted from fresh bricks of parmesan and Romano cheeses and salamis retrieved from a large refrigerator. The aroma of fresh sauce, Italian sausage, and meatballs wafts out into the dining room where white linen tablecloths cover the massive oak table.

One of my new friends in our predominantly Italian neighborhood has extended an invitation for me to "break bread" with her family on a Sunday afternoon. Mary Ann's grandfather stands at the head of the table and blesses our meal, where I am transported to a foreign country with one word, "Abbandanza," meaning plentiful and abundant.

Our meal ends with a serving of spumoni and cheesecake served with fresh strawberries and cream. After much coaxing, my grandmother agrees to teach me the basics, so I can extend an invitation to my new friend.

Before long, I'm rolling out fresh dough, cutting up root

vegetables for delicious stews, and peeling and slicing apples for her cinnamon apple pies. All this time, I am learning about my family in County Cork, Ireland, and their journey to America as immigrants.

Sunday finally arrives and we are all seated at the kitchen table, dining on baked ham and scalloped potatoes, corned beef and cabbage, fresh rolls, and my grandmother's warm apple pie, served with a dollop of vanilla ice cream. After clearing the table, we share stories of Italy and Ireland, where generations ago our stories began.

I listen for the sound of the motorcycle's roar as it races into our driveway every evening, skidding to a stop on the asphalt. Our downstairs neighbor is a police officer with two boys who attend school with me.

With my family's permission, I embark on my first bike ride. Seated on the back, my heart races. To seal the deal, I quickly make the sign of the cross on my forehead, secure my helmet, and hold on for dear life to the straps on the policeman's bulky leather jacket.

The engine roars to life beneath me like a proud stallion huffing loudly, snorting and pawing the ground. Coaxed into submission, the bike gentles itself for the young inexperienced rider on the back. A heady sense of freedom rockets me into another dimension, where time stands still and my spirit takes flight.

Climbing the hilly streets in our neighborhood, we pass by the church and school I attend. Whizzing down a side street,

I spy a familiar store front with a display of chocolates and penny candy in the window. Angelo, the shop owner provides our neighborhood with homemade lemon ice on hot summer nights.

Arriving back home, I carefully dismount to avoid the hot metal sides. Looking up, I see my grandfather in the window smiling down at me, bestowing me with a thumbs up for approval.

Piano Man

Following my father's departure, we move to a flat on the north side of the city to live with my maternal grandparents, Thomas and Hannah Kenney. My sense of belonging and safety is dependent on their ability to create a loving and nurturing environment for me, while my mother works full time to support us.

My grandfather met his bride while working as a brick layer in New York City. He is quite a charmer with sky blue eyes and a mischievous grin. In a cherished photograph, he stands with his coworkers on either side, perched on a scaffold several stories off the ground, looking like an accomplished tightrope walker.

He is quickly replacing Steve McQueen as my idol, but later in life, a man named Bill Wilson will take center stage. My stately Irish grandmother has earned quite the reputation for her outstanding cooking and baking skills. An assortment of wide-brimmed hats adorned with silk flowers and embroidered with lace sets off her dimples, high cheek bones, and Irish complexion.

Sunday afternoon she can be seen strolling in the neighborhood, wearing one of her lovely picture hats and chatting up the neighbors along the way. While her family reaps the rewards, she's sought out to cater weddings, showers, reunions, and even funerals—especially the sometimes rowdy Irish wakes, where grief is measured by the pint.

Years later, she takes a fall down the wooden stairs leading to the basement. After a stroke leaves her with one side of her face twitching constantly, her beautiful hats are donated to a worthy cause and her smile is never quite the same.

Throughout this time, there was no mention of my father, even though I saw unopened letters on the hutch in his writing. My father worked as a landscaper and had quite a talent for the piano. However, jazz, blues and booze halted any dreams he might have entertained of playing professionally.

Encouraged by my love for music, my mother purchases a small black Wurlitzer piano, which takes center stage in the parlor of our second-story flat. She arranges for private piano lessons at the school where I attend fifth grade.

Windows are open on this sultry summer day. As I climb the steep hill leading to our flat, the familiar sound of a piano playing on the second floor catches my attention. Arriving with my sheet music in hand, I open the apartment door to discover my father seated at my piano, tickling the ivories with the strong smell of alcohol surrounding him like an impenetrable fog.

I retreat to my bedroom to wait for the all clear, signaling my father's departure. Then I rush to the landing to catch a glimpse of his wistful face gazing back at me, while he is again whisked away in a van. I am left with so many unanswered questions.

Some time later, inebriated and unable to navigate the small rowboat back to shore, my paternal grandfather drowned in a popular lake. Back then, the body had to be identified by a family member and the police brought the body to the house for identification. How heartbreaking that must have been.

The word alcoholism was never mentioned in my home, but I knew there was something in my life that set me apart from my classmates. With few friends, I spent much of those early years alone creating an imaginary, happy family with my dolls and diary—a family that included my father. The seeds of my father's disease that were firmly planted in my young psyche would sprout later in my own life and lead me down a heartbreaking path.

One night after searching for hours, the authorities find my father lying unconscious at the side of the road not far from a liquor store. On my father's death certificate, the cause of death is listed as "acute alcohol poisoning." My father's condition was to remain a deep, dark secret for many years to come.

Nunsense

Hurrying to the back of the bus on a rainy Monday morning, I tug at the ugly rubbers worn over my new "Buster Brown" shoes, releasing them with a loud snap. My shoes are an expensive purchase and must be protected from the elements. I had pleaded for the "penny" loafers so popular that school year, but to no avail.

Making the transition from middle school to high school is monumental. I stuff the rubbers into my book bag (my new best friend) with my lunch consisting of a PB and J sandwich, crunchy celery filled with artificial cheese spread, an apple, two chocolate chip cookies, and two paper napkins.

I can already feel the tension in the air. The staccato of their functional black shoes announces their arrival. I can hear the swish of the bulky underskirts layered under their floor-length black habit, as they patrol up and down each aisle monitoring the start of our exams.

Mustering all the courage of a tufted tit mouse, I follow the arrow leading to my new homeroom. Tripping over a mine field of curved metal legs attached to rows of perfectly positioned desks, I stumble up the aisle to the familiar laughter and snickering of the parochial schoolboys whispering and pointing at me.

Sliding into my seat, perspiration begins to pool at the neck of my perky Peter Pan collar, and I tug at the narrow tie I am forced to wear. Some of the boys (bullies) could wear a hole in the carpeting, walking the plank to Mother Superior's office on a regular basis. The nuns pounce on them as they pass notes back and forth. One by one down the hall they'd go with a snicker on their faces.

The sound of the nun's ruler making contact with a troublesome boy disturbs the quiet. A mischievous boy (future juvenile delinquent) is slapped on the hand twice with the wooden ruler and I flinch as a nun delivers the blow. My heart is pounding as I stare at the clock on the wall, preparing myself to bolt out of the room at any moment when the preordained alarm echoes throughout the school.

Four Eyes Meets Piano Legs

A few of the more bald-faced boys confiscate my purse, tying it to the window sash and dangling it out the second-story window. I search everywhere for my purse, but without my glasses, I'm clueless. Shortly before the nun arrives back in the classroom, one of the boys approaches me. He hands over the evidence with a smarmy smirk on his face mumbling, "Is this what you're looking for?"

After that experience, I never take off my glasses in school again. If the measles has stamped me, the inability to fit in and make lasting friends defines me.

Across the aisle, a girl transferring from another school smiles and then quickly looks away when the boys start acting up. Seen through the haze of a magnetized myopia of rejection, I close my eyes and wish myself anywhere but here.

Seated at the end of the lunch table, I quickly learn how cruel the boys can be. Two words are spoken, echoing through the cafeteria on my first day. Swiftly I gather up my lunch bag and hurry back to the empty classroom. "Four Eyes" becomes a new mantra and follows me around like an appendage.

Transitioning from "Four Eyes" into "Book Worm," I spend most of my free time and weekends devouring books. Saturdays are challenging, as my mother now works five days a week and uses the weekends to catch up on her housework.

The vacuum cleaner is a loud belcher and when it bangs into my closed bedroom door, I know it's time to get up. I remember a particularly dulled-down day with gray skies and a soft rain falling. My mother is catching up on some paperwork from the office and I am buried in my new library book, *The Secret Garden.* Propped up on my pillows, I am in my own world and already fast forwarding on a journey worthy of Harry Potter himself.

One Saturday morning stands out, when my mother knocks on my bedroom door. As years slip away, she shares her own experience as a young girl branded "Piano Legs."

In that small room, soft light turns to shadow as we continue to talk. I learn of a young girl who decides to rise above the name calling. She channels her energy into befriending some of the not so popular girls and over the course of four years, they form lasting bonds.

I begin to smile as she tells me how she learned to laugh with herself and not at herself. She made a decision that took her out of the role of a victim.

That Monday morning, I arrive at school early with a new confidence. Approaching a few of the girls, I listen as they tell me their challenges, so like mine. Exchanging phone numbers, favorite book titles, music, and gossiping (mostly about boys and certain teachers), a sisterhood is formed. Thus, the journey into adulthood begins in earnest.

Dream a Little Dream

A dream is taking shape as my mother works the drive-through window. Mom has been hoping to find a property where we can all have our own space. With a daughter on the cusp of her teenage years and two aging parents in deteriorating health, an opportunity presents itself to her.

The house behind the bank is going to be razed and sold to enlarge the parking lot, so my mother puts a purchase offer on the property. The one stipulation is that she will need to move the house from its current location. The house is located on a lot at the bottom of a steep hill.

The year is 1955, and back in the day, this is a grand adventure. Our neighborhood is all abuzz at the sight of this carefully engineered caravan ferrying a small Cape Cod style house down the street.

Imagine this ... my mother, a decisive and no-nonsense woman in her two-piece tweed suit and black pumps standing in the road at the bottom of a steep hill. As the house approaches, she is waving her arms like a great conductor.

Sleep-deprived children heading to the bus stop to gawk, and neighbors peer from behind lace curtains to see what all the commotion is about.

A few days later, my mother arrives home from work with the daily newspaper displaying a photo of the scene. In my mind's eye, she will always be a champion for positive change and affirmative action, while shaping her own path and bringing people together, like the community organizer she is.

On our enclosed front porch, I read by the lamplight until my eyelids droop and the words begin to blur on the page. Early Sunday morning, the neighborhood awakens to the sound of Dominic, our paperboy, speeding by on his Schwinn bike, while hurling newspapers onto front porches and stoops. His performance is so good that you can set the alarm by the whack of the paper as it strikes the steps.

When my aunt and uncle come over on Sunday afternoons to play Canasta and Pinochle, I kneel next to the register in my bedroom, listening to their conversation. and the sound of laughter. It feels like our new house is healing all of us from the inside out.

Now a teenager and forming new friendships, pajama parties are all the rage. My friend, Joanne, and I alternate our sleepovers on Friday nights. My mother makes popcorn in a large aluminum pot and serves it with melted butter. On Saturday morning, we'd awaken to the aroma of her fresh blueberry or apple pancakes drizzled with real maple syrup and crispy bacon strips.

We'd spend our evenings combing through *Teen Magazine* and *Seventeen* for the latest makeup and hairstyles. We'd read *Photoplay* and *Modern Screen* from cover to cover while searching for our dream date. Who wouldn't love to ride in a convertible with Steve McQueen or gaze into Tony Curtis' bedroom eyes! When I begin dating, my mother switches the porch light on and off, using her own "Morse Code," signaling the time to say goodnight.

Over time, the grass is planted, a border of carnations and marigolds line the side yard, and a cement birdbath appears, complete with chirping birds refreshing themselves in the cool water. My grandfather grows strawberries, and we picnic in the shade of two stately evergreen trees in the back.

Mastering the art of grilling on our Hibachi, my mother prepares her all-beef hot dogs and sirloin burgers. The aroma carries on the breeze, reminding everyone the lazy, hazy days of summer are finally here.

The sound of my alarm clock jars me awake. My clock radio announces that schools have been closed and businesses are shuttered, as a major snowstorm and howling wind invade central New York. As the snow rapidly piles up on the roadways and sidewalks, emergency road crews work arduously to keep up with Mother Nature's assault.

What an adventure this turns out to be as my mother and I take turns shoveling. The welcome heat pouring out of the register on the floor warms my stiff fingers and achy toes. My scarf and mittens, caked with crusty snow, thaw out and my grandmother puts my hands under her ample armpits to warm them.

Too soon, the unwelcome jarring of the alarm clock announces "Business as Usual" and school is back in session.

Home alone, an opportunity presents itself to me. Teenage curiosity and a bit of rebellion lead me to the basement where Pandora's box awaits hidden in a dark corner. Small keepsakes and a punch bowl set are layered between tissue paper and old newspapers in a cardboard box labeled "KEEP."

Discovering a record in a sleeve with the name Robert printed on it, I hurry back to my bedroom. I carefully place the record on the platter, positioning the needle and gently releasing it. The quality of the record is tinny and faded, yet something about the sound appeals to me.

Someone To Watch Over Me is a melody that has haunted me. The compelling melody performed on piano brings back a memory of my mother humming it to me as a small child. The artist is my own father. Here in the privacy of my bedroom, a piece of the puzzle that is my father falls into place.

Buzz Off

My grandparents are the two people responsible for bringing Aunt Sarah into our lives. As a young girl, Aunt Sarah had been placed in an orphanage due to a tragic fire that erupted in the tenement where she lived. A pot of boiling water fell off the stove and severely burned one of her siblings. Both her sibling and her mother perished in the fire. Unable to cope, her father placed her in an orphanage and walked away.

My mother and uncle welcomed Aunt Sarah into their home as a member of the family and as a cousin through marriage. Years later, my Aunt Sarah shared a story with me of when she came to live with her aunt and uncle.

My mother's name is Sarah Jane. Because Sarah would be coming to live with them, she began calling herself "Jane" to help my Aunt Sarah adapt to her new family. Sarah, a feisty and tenacious girl, soon earned the name "Tomboy" among her classmates and could stand up to the best of them.

My grandfather was the one who traveled by train to New

York and brought Sarah home. He took Aunt Sarah to his favorite barber to have her hair trimmed. Sporting a new cut hidden under her cap, she entered the classroom and sat down at her desk. One of the boys yelled out, "Who are you?" Her reply was, "It's me, Sarah, and **what's it to ya!**"

She loved telling the story of how this persistent soldier in uniform was determined to be introduced to her at the brewery where she worked in the office. She was very distrustful and reluctant to allow Uncle Art to "court" her.

She had learned to be tough and made no bones about putting him in his place. He was informed in no uncertain terms, "I have no intentions of getting married, and if I ever do, it certainly won't be to you!" If the war had been tough, it had certainly prepared him for this Irish colleen.

She informed Grandma when she came home from her first date with Arthur that she had laughed so hard that her sides ached. He, in turn, went home to tell his mother that he had met the girl he was going to marry. I have photographs of their wedding day and feisty or not, he sure made Aunt Sarah incredibly happy. They didn't agree about everything though. While he watched westerns with John Wayne, she just adored Elvis Presley. So it was *Happy Trails to You* and *Are You Lonesome Tonight* merging. One of Aunt Sarah's favorite expressions was, "Buzz off!" When Uncle Art would tease her and act up about dinner, she would say, "Eat it or wear it!" "I'll knock your block off" was another endearing quote.

Growing up in my grandparent's Irish Catholic household was where Aunt Sarah honed her talent for commentary (solicited or not). Aunt Sarah could shop all day on Saturdays and my grandparents often said, "Arthur has the patience of Job." I always thought that Job was some long-lost relative that I had yet to meet.

Later, after reading in the Bible about Job being tested by God over and over, I had a greater appreciation for the wisdom of patience. Aunt Sarah admittedly was not always patient.

One Sunday morning after returning from church, she was rolling out dough for a piecrust and it just wasn't cooperating. Uncle Art heard her struggling in the kitchen and he yelled out (from his favorite armchair in the living room where he had a good sightline into the kitchen), "Sarah, do you need my help?"

Her reply: "If I needed your help, I'd ask for it." Uttering a few choice words, she hurled that piecrust at the wall. Later, I heard that Uncle Art stated, "Why that's the best peach pie I've ever tasted."

Aunt Sarah shared a story with me on her 85th birthday. While looking through boxes of old photographs, we were listening to Cole Porter tunes from a movie on television. She and Uncle Art were very seldom apart, and she had always wanted to travel after retirement. She had planned an extensive trip through Europe with a group from her church parish.

Uncle Art simply couldn't work up the enthusiasm to

travel. Possibly he had seen enough during his tour of duty with the Army. He sent her off with his blessings. He looked forward to his westerns with John Wayne, Gene Autry, and Roy Rogers, and to his nightly beer. He'd dine at the restaurant in a home next to their building and where the specialty was always "Polenta."

Aunt Sarah returned two weeks later and there was Uncle Art greeting her at the airport. Picking up the bags from the terminal, he turned and smiled saying, "Where would you like us to go next?" From that time on, they would "travel the road side by side."

Are You Being Served?

Aunt Sarah brings desserts and Uncle Art arrives with a six pack of beer on holidays and special occasions. Uncle Art shares his own version of **fractured fairy tales** with us, regaling us with the story of *Goldilocks and the Three Beers.*" While they never have children of their own, my aunt and uncle have more than enough room in their hearts for all of us.

The night before Thanksgiving, friends and family members are booted out of the kitchen. We play board games like Monopoly and card games like Michigan Rummy. Grandma would be preparing her famous pies. Always a favorite is my grandmother's mile-high lemon meringue pie, tart and fluffy from the egg whites she skillfully beats into the metal bowl.

Grandma would be up late that night preparing her turkey and mixing all the ingredients for her famous stuffing. Whenever you ask Grandma for her recipes, she simply says, "I put in a pinch of this and a dab of that." The aromas entice me and the easy comfort lulls me to sleep. The warmth from the kitchen permeates our house and we all awake refreshed and eager to begin our feast.

My chore is to mash the potatoes, adding just enough heated milk and butter. The table is heaped with casseroles of green beans and sweet potatoes and fluffy mashed potatoes. There are candied apples and a relish tray brimming with green olives, sweet pickles, celery stuffed with pimento cheese, and corn relish. Two bowls of turkey gravy are placed on the table, one with giblets and another without, in gleaming silver boats to be ladled out.

My Irish grandfather plays a part in the festivities, too. While everyone is bustling around the kitchen on Thanksgiving morning, he takes himself out of the fray. He walks down to Angelo's corner bar to share a brew with the other patrons who have been shooed out of the house.

My grandmother would accompany Uncle Art and bring meals to a few of our housebound neighbors. By now my grandfather has returned from his jaunt, sprawled out on the rug in the hallway between the coat closet and bathroom. With a beatific smile on his face and arms crossed, he resembles the turkey we are about to eat! When I whisper to my grandmother that "I need to use the bathroom," her reply is, "Oh, just step over him."

My grandfather has an Irish heart, filled with mischief and funny jokes he is only too eager to share. I see him with a broad smile sharing a drink with our neighbors, and happy and at ease without a drink, as well.

However, my memories of my father are sketchy. Without his presence in my life, he remains a lonely man who just could not go without a drink. It was as though his very existence depended on alcohol.

Christmas Day arrives and, flinging off the covers, I race down the stairs in bare feet. Only a few crumbs remain on the plate where two Toll House chocolate chip cookies were carefully arranged the night before. Not even a trace is left of the warm milk in our Christmas mug. Surely Santa has been here!

I seem to have more presents to open than anyone, so I begin by carefully removing the green velvet bow on a beautifully wrapped box. Parting the tissue paper, I am surprised to find a nightgown in a lovely shade of pink. It will be years before I can wear it! Across town, Aunt Shirley opens a package containing a beautiful Madame Alexander doll that is meant for me. It's soon sorted out and I am sure this story will be played forward for many years to come.

The formal dining room table is set for the adults. In the front room, two card tables are placed side by side, covered with a long festive tablecloth for younger cousins and friends. We're treated to chilled shrimp cocktail served in a glass dish with cocktail sauce on the side.

There is laughter and nervous giggling as we pass the fancy sterling silver tray heaped with stuffed celery, sweet pickles, and large black and green olives. While passing the tray, something runs amuck and the tray tilts, scattering monstrous runaway olives across the floor like miniature bowling balls. Order is quickly restored after we quickly stuff the evidence into our gaping mouths.

While the adults have their coffee and desserts around the dining room table, we politely ask to be excused and venture outdoors to release pent up energy. Our coats and gloves are no match for the temperature, and soon we're driven inside by the bone-chilling cold.

Returning to our table, mugs of hot cocoa with marshmallows melting on top greet us and mysteriously, a deck of cards materializes. My fun-loving mother winks at me as she clears the table. Thoughtful and caring, her gesture provides us with many hours of entertainment.

Soon the evening comes to an end. Accompanied by the sound of my grandfather's soft steady snoring in the next room, I slip into a deep winter slumber.

Some Enchanted Evening

Wearing her faux fur Persian lamb jacket and matching chapeau, my mother stands out in the crowd as a steady stream of patrons fill the foyer, sounding more like a swarm of droning bees. With a whiff of my mother's Chanel No. 5 perfume, red woolen coat, and knee-high patent leather boots, I fancy myself quite the sophisticate.

With the orchestra tuning up in the pit, we join the queue waiting to be seated. This evening's performance of the *Nutcracker Suite* ballet is my introduction to the classics. With Christmas just two weeks away, what an enchanted evening it proves to be. Twirling ballerinas in dazzling costumes, marching toy soldiers sporting uniforms of vibrant red, blue and gold, and pixie-like fairies enchant the audience, casting a spell over us all.

Exiting the theater, the night air is cold and crisp, and the popular Caramel Corn Shop provides a perfect ending. I watch through the storefront window as a woman wearing a long white apron stirs a vat containing melted caramel with a long wooden paddle.

Spicy candied cinnamon apples individually wrapped in festive cellophane resting on the glass countertop greet the customers. The aroma of caramel and cinnamon waft out the door down a narrow alleyway leading to the backstage door of the theater.

My exposure to theater broadens over the next ten years, when we attend Pulitzer Prize winning plays and Broadway shows held at the Landmark, Syracuse Stage, and Civic Center. Songs from *Camelot, South Pacific,* and *Carousel* are performed by outstanding performers. Without this exposure to drama and music, my own budding creativity and imagination might never have taken flight.

I remember kneeling on the floor of our living room when Ed Sullivan introduces a talented group from Liverpool, England. In a state of near ecstasy, I am carried away and swept up by the phenomenon of Beatlemania. *Money, Yellow Submarine, Twist and Shout, A Hard Day's Night,* and *Get Back* are part of the revolution for young singers and dancers to take to the streets and "shake their own tambourines." I must be a part of it! Lawrence Welk fades into the distance and for the first time, my mother and I part company in our musical choices.

Our cruise ship docks in Nassau and after a day scootering around on the island, we embark on a night of "clubbing." My coworker and I have embarked on a cruise to Bermuda. We plan to enjoy every minute!

Our third night brings us to a popular night spot in Bermuda located in a cave. The atmosphere is electric. With almost every Beatles song memorized and feeling confident, I charm the band into allowing me to sing, *If I Give My Heart to You*, as my chosen slow song.

I must have done well, because loud cheering and clapping ensues when I finish. Of course, it helps that most of the crowd is slightly tipsy and lighthearted. Escorted back to the ship by a few of our fellow passengers, we pass out on our bunks.

A rough sea and dreadful hangover keep me in the room for most of the next day. The following night, we dine at the captain's table and after winning a dance contest, I find myself in the officer's quarters late at night making out.

Slightly disheveled and disoriented, I stagger down the corridor back to my room with my reputation and virginity still intact. What begins as fun with my love affair with booze soon becomes fun with problems, and then eventually, just problems.

Reaching this stage, I arrive at what is referred to as the "jumping off point." My mother is the one who suffers the most, as she witnesses the destructive path her only child is embarking on.

Alcoholism reflects my father's handsome face gazing back at me in the mirror, long before my mother met him many years ago. Like-minded kindred spirits, we are powerless over its force.

New York, New York

As a fledgling driver, my mother forbids me to turn on the radio to avoid any distractions. One year later and still mindful of her surroundings, a confident and capable driver welcomes the station broadcasting the Big Band sounds. We've been invited to the "Big Apple" for a long weekend to visit our extended family.

Living in crowded neighborhoods with limited parking space, our relatives live in high-rise apartment buildings and ride the subways to work every day.

The communities in New York are ripe with the aromas and colors of each ethnic region. The neighborhoods are a virtual United Nations of Irish Catholics residing in a predominately Italian neighborhood, around the corner from a Jewish deli.

My aunt and uncle have two daughters who are about four years apart. Both my cousins live at home and work in the city. My younger cousin is soft-spoken with warm brown eyes, a nurse at a well-esteemed hospital, while my older cousin is the sophisticate, a buyer for a major department store in Manhattan.

On a beautiful Saturday morning, my mother, cousins, and I are heading into Manhattan. My mother takes my hand as we make our way down into the subway tunnel. There is an otherworldly feel to this place and, as we pass through the turnstile, there's little time for fear or trepidation boarding the already crowded car.

Suddenly the train lurches as we stand with our feet firmly planted. My feet barely touch the ground as I am propelled forward by the frantic, frenzied stream of commuters jockeying into position at the exits. Now, at street level, I'm assaulted by the smells and sounds of the big city

A billowing puff of hot air rises from the pavement, taking my light summer skirt for a ride. I yank it down below my knees as the light quickly changes. The traffic police blow their whistles for the pedestrians to cross the street. Taxi cabs screech to a halt, blasting their horns in frustration at the gawking, slow-moving crowd.

The window displays highlight an assortment of Italian leather shoes and handbags. My cousin is our guide, pointing out the latest fashions from London, Boston, and Paris. Fashionable dresses and lingerie from Paris, and woolen pantsuits with matching vests and tailored trench coats from London are all the rage. An endless parade of women descend on the jewelry stores and perfume counters beckoning to them.

One of the highlights of my day is a surprise, a luncheon at the popular Schrafft's restaurant. The menu features a special tuna salad plate with fresh fruit and croissants. They also serve date and nut bread with cream cheese and tomato rarebit on toast. We finish off with hot fudge sundaes with warm fudge sauce, whipped cream, and chopped walnuts.

For most of the walk back to the subway, I remain in a sugar-induced fog. The sway of the car and click clack of the wheels lulls me into a dreamless sleep on our journey back to the Bronx.

Let Me Entertain You

The scene is set; Friday night in October in the basement of the Catholic Church we attend where our first eighth-grade dance will take place.

My best friend and I descend the steep concrete steps leading into the hall. Approaching the crime scene, the sound of laughter makes me wonder what I have gotten myself into. Taking a deep breath and giddy with nerves, we stride into the arena.

The parochial schoolboys are either lined up against the wall or crowded around the punch bowl. Snacks are arranged on a long table covered with pastel paper table-cloths. On the opposite side, the girls wearing their poodle skirts, cardigan sweater sets, and saddle shoes whisper among themselves while checking us out.

We have practiced some of the latest dances in our basement almost every weekend. Soon my friend is dancing the jitterbug with her partner, a boy who just recently transferred to our school. Left standing with a small group of girls, but wishing to be singled out for at least one dance (hopefully a fast one), my toes are tapping to the beat.

Suddenly one of the boys sidles across the room, eyes locked on mine, and moves in for the kill. Being escorted out on the dance floor is a heady feeling and a slow song is playing. Suddenly, a paper grocer bag is placed over my head. Ripping the bag off my head, I look around to witness the shocked faces of my classmates. Beyond humiliated and cheeks red with the embarrassment, I remember my mother's words to me and take a stand.

Rather than departing in utter defeat, I remain. That night becomes a turning point for me. There are very few times when I am singled out in a negative way after that.

As it turns out, the expression, "What goes around comes around," proves to be true. The girls have been whispering among themselves and pull me aside to share a secret. The boys involved have been bullied for their nicknames (unmentionable here) and their reputations set them up for failure that night. Their "dance cards" will remain empty.

My mother and mentor advises me to "rise above it." I am already learning how valuable this phrase will be as I mature into a woman.

Good Grief

My mother relies on public transportation until a time when my grandfather becomes ill. Diagnosed with cancer, he is moved to a nursing home not far from the bank where Mom works. Prior to signing up for driving lessons, she purchases a reliable compact car. With just three driving lessons under her belt, she's good to go.

Later, the medical community is baffled at the remission of an aggressive cancer in such an elderly man. Now he can return home for a few more years. Without his strong faith and abiding love for his creator, it's doubtful that he would have had more time to be with us.

However, one day he is taken to the hospital. This time, when my mother returns from visiting him, she stands in the doorway and tells us that my grandfather has passed away. The only sound in this hollow place is the metronome of my grandfather's cuckoo clock hanging on the wall nearby.

Hoping to feel some comfort, I kneel by my grandmother's chair and put my head in her lap. Our Irish Catholic family can be described as stoic when it comes to showing emotions and I long for some sign that crying is permitted. There must be a deep well where tears are stored for times like these, but how do I locate it?

Announcing the hour, the cuckoo clock startles me. Without any response from my grandmother, I slip away, retreating to the comfort of my bedroom. Mom makes all the necessary phone calls and begins the process of arranging for the wake and funeral to follow.

Hoping to feel a sense of his presence, I steal into my grandfather's room. His bureau becomes a still life of all he holds dear. A crocheted runner covers the oak dresser, where a bristle brush and little black comb, two cotton hankies perfectly folded, a small bank book, and his well-worn wooden rosary beads remain.

Later that night, I awake to the sound of muffled crying. My mother is finally releasing her pent-up tears. Now I understand the whispering I'd hear in the next room while getting ready for school early in the morning. I wish I could freeze-frame the picture of my grandfather kneeling at the side of his bed reciting his prayers.

Where All the Lights Are Bright

Looking forward to an uneventful summer after graduation, I secure employment as an office worker in a well-established manufacturing plant. I meet a few like-minded girls who attend business school. After becoming proficient in shorthand and typing classes to increase speed and accuracy, I learn some new rules. Along with advancing from stenographer to a secretarial position, the new rules are as follows:

Work hard and make a good impression.

Learn to party.

Lastly, the golden rule—always have a date on a Saturday night. If you don't, spend every Wednesday night out seeking a date for Saturday night, with Friday night set aside for dancing the night away.

My first experience with Rule 2 begins when Petula Clark's popular song, *Downtown*, lures me into a murky, mysterious, and hypnotic dance club with my friends. Awakening to the throbbing, pulsing music, my first Manhattan cocktail warms me to the core, offering me a false sense of security and relieving me of the bondage of self.

In an altered state, alcohol soon becomes a subtle, seductive lover and a constant, compelling force in my life. The stronger the drink, the sooner I am convinced that I've found the solution to my inhibited, self-conscious nature. With a newly formed personality, my social status greatly improves, and a door opens where I'm pursued by handsome men.

My relationship with alcohol takes center stage in my life. Broadening my horizons, I fly to Miami on spring break with my college girlfriends. We vacation in Lake George with co-workers, all pleasure seekers and kindred spirits in our enjoyment of dancing and partying.

Early on, there are very few consequences to my being inebriated. On the surface, my life appears manageable, and appearances are everything. It's all fun, other than a severe sunburn and sun poisoning from passing out on the sands of Miami Beach. This trip includes a visit to the ER, antibiotics, and long baking soda baths in the tub for the remainder of my trip. At this point, my reputation isn't tainted by alcohol.

Regrets ... I've Had a Few

On a weekend trip to the Adirondack Mountains with friends from work, we party hard until the stroke of midnight. Then we meet some good-looking college students who have rented a house in the village.

Following them back to their house, the party continues. Raised an Irish Catholic girl with a somewhat strict upbringing in matters sexual, and schooled by a "no nonsense" order of nuns who supervise my every thought, I remain a virgin.

At this house party, I am told later that I passed out on the sofa. After trying to awaken me several times, my friends leave me there, cautioning one of the guys to keep an eye on me. It's now morning and I've slept through the night while he sits like a sentinel in a nearby chair all night long.

Imagine this ... he cares more for me than I care for myself and keeps his commitment. Without him, I could easily have been taken advantage of by one or all of the four guys sleeping it off in the bedrooms upstairs … but not on his watch. Wherever you are; THANK YOU!

During this time, I'm still living in my mother's home with my aging grandmother. After her tragic fall down the cellar stairs and the devastating stroke that follows, our family dynamics have changed drastically.

My grandmother's world shrinks to the main floor of our house, as she can no longer climb the stairs to her bedroom. She now sleeps on a single bed that resides in our dining room. My mother has an addition built off our kitchen for a small bathroom.

Little is expected of me, and little is offered. This continues my "It's all about me" phase and it lasts far too long. Years later, I'm faced with some of my deepest regrets.

Alcoholics are often unable to form relationships. Instead, they take hostages, rarely looking back at the "wreckage of the past" unless forced to.

One of my most profound regrets happens while my mother is still working, as well as caring for my grandmother. She has an important business commitment in New York and has asked me to be home in time before her trip. I would need to be there until the visiting nurse arrives in the morning. Her flight is at 6:30 am with the taxi scheduled to pick her up at 4:00 am.

Of course, I promise to be there *well* before that time. Earlier that evening, I meet my blind date in the lobby of a trendy hotel and popular spot for dancing and socializing.

My date happens to work at the same bank where my mother is employed. She has cautioned me about his reputation as a heavy drinker and being a lady's man. Of course, this intrigues me even more.

With only bar snacks to sustain me, fortified by several martinis and several sexy moves on the dance floor, my resistance to his charm dwindles. I find myself in a room on the third floor at midnight.

After "fooling around" for a while, my underwear and slip remain my only grasp on sanity. I blurt out, "I am still a virgin!"

This statement unleashes a torrent of words like, "wasted a room" and "you can find your own way home, bitch." An alarm clock on the table between the two beds separating us flashes the time like a neon sign.

Startled awake by the loud snoring in the bed next to me, I frantically search for my clothes. With just a half hour left before the witching hour, I arrange for a taxi and arrive home just in time to see my mother's cab turning the corner.

At exactly 4:00 am, I answer the knock on the door announcing the arrival of my grandmother's nurse. Grandma's health has been deteriorating since my grandfather's death, so my mother carries an added burden on her heart. God intervenes in a way that brings peace to my mother and Grandma passes away quietly in her sleep.

My self-absorbed and self-seeking behavior offers little

security for my mother—once again, I have let her down. As a young adult living rent free in my mother's home, I now realize the added stress I have piled on to her already challenging life.

Weekends for me are a time for late nights, spending days at the beach tanning and preening like a sleek cat, partying until last call is announced. Sometimes I even head home in a stranger's car when my friends make the sensible decision to leave earlier.

Possessing little emotional maturity, alcohol stunts my growth, but I am incapable of facing the truth. Alcohol has become my relationship of choice and I have no desire to look within.

Regrettably, I realize how much worry, anxiety, and pain I've caused my family and friends due to my inability to accept responsibility for myself as an adult. Yet, while I am becoming my father's daughter, alcohol licks my wounds just fine ... thank you very much!

Landing at the airport in Honolulu during the Christmas season, I am greeted by a lighted sign above the entrance. "Mele Kalikimaka" is the Hawaiian phrase for Merry Christmas and my soon-to-be fiancée meets me at baggage claim area.

After shipping out for basic training prior to being deployed to Viet Nam, our letters take on a new intimacy. Shortly after arriving at his friend's apartment on base, he presents me with a lovely engagement ring. While I am surprised, I accept the gift and the commitment it represents immediately.

I haven't been engaged before, so now, at twenty years of age, it seems fitting. While our time together is short, we take a jeep and visit the island of Oahu. We stay with a married couple, and we sleep together on the sleeper sofa in the living room. The couple are still in their honeymoon phase, so it feels like an invasion of their privacy and awkward to be sleeping together when I refuse to have sex.

I haven't come all this way to throw away my precious virginity, although it surely might have comforted my anxious army recruit. It would be like attempting to break into Fort Knox to remove the tight girdle I wear to bed every night.

Arriving home, I immediately put the ring in my jewelry box like a trophy. While we correspond lovingly through letters, I am back on the dating scene.

Thankfully, he arrives back in Syracuse with no physical harm, but the war has taken its toll on his peace of mind and ability to readjust. It doesn't help when I return the ring and disengage myself from our relationship shortly thereafter.

I hadn't wanted to hurt him while he was away and honestly should never have taken the ring in the first place. Caught up in the romance and excitement of the moment, I sober up quickly when thinking about the consequences of waiting for his return.

My mother says little about my quick decision and

ability to detach emotionally. However, I know I hadn't been honest with myself or my rejected fiancée. Fortified by a certain amount of disgrace and guilt, my search for a drinking partner now begins in earnest.

ALCOHOLISM
... A LOVE STORY

Sarah Jane and Patty Ann
(wearing those coke bottle glasses)

To Sir with Love

The "Poor House North" is where I meet my first husband, John. One of my coworkers arranges a "blind" date for us. Wearing his Air Force uniform, he stands out in the thickening crowd of rebel rousers. Tall, slender, handsome, and a dead ringer for "Broadway Joe Namath," he leans over at the bar and picks up a drink, then walks towards me. This Air Force captain has me hook, line, and sinker—just eight months later, we marry and settle down in our first apartment.

We agree on getting a puppy and drive out to a breeder in the country where we meet Sir Andrew, or "Andy" as we affectionately call him. Andy captures our hearts as he sidesteps and bounces his way toward us. He is a gorgeous, magnificent creature, but we know little to nothing about this breed. All we know is that he is an AKC-registered St. Bernard pup with all his papers. Had we really looked at the size of the paws on this pup, we'd have realized how large he would grow to be.

I had never seen Sarah Jane with a dog before and, while

she certainly relishes the idea of a grandchild, Andy takes center stage for almost six years! There are many mishaps and blunders along the way. He has no sense of his size or weight. He thinks nothing of climbing up on the couch and throwing himself across your lap.

Picture this scene—we are hosting a party for my husband's peers who work at the hospital where he is newly employed. I am in the kitchen preparing drinks when I hear loud, almost hysterical laughter coming from the living room.

Sir Andrew had skirted the dining room table, bounding into the living room to lunge spread-eagle over the coffee table. Then he begins devouring the delicious homemade cheeseball I had made that morning, scattering crackers and a tin of mixed nuts all over the carpet.

Like my mother, Andy is particularly fond of ice cream. When I place a disposable aluminum pie tin on the kitchen floor, he works that dish around the room into all the corners, lapping up every single creamy melted drop. My mother always brings a half-gallon of his favorite vanilla custard ice cream to share with her "Grand Dog" over the weekend.

Andy manages to win over anyone who encounters him. His displays of affection include jumping up and putting his rather large paws on shoulders.

St. Bernard's are kind, compassionate, and terrified of authority figures—especially anyone wearing a white coat. Driving to the veterinarian's office with Andy in the back seat provides our first clue of just how fearful he is, despite his intimidating size.

This is the middle of a long winter in central New York, shortly after a large dump of snow is hardening on the pavement as the temperature drops. Sly as a fox, Sir Andrew makes his move and squeezes out of the car before we can collar him. What a sight!

My always cool, calm, collected mother is pursuing him, dressed in her mid-length winter coat and high heels. I watch as she straddles Andy like a pony while trying to keep him from slipping down the hill and into the swiftly moving water in the creek behind the vet's office.

I race inside, alerting two of the male staff, who hurry outside, lift him up in their strong arms, and calmly carry him into the office. Andy's eyes are sad and mournful as he gazes back at us. However, in the next few years, he becomes confident and trusting of the staff. He lumbers into the office on his own steam, eager to receive the treats offered for being such a good dog.

After purchasing our first home in the North Country, our neighbor observes my husband being dragged down the hill behind our house, trying to gain control of our dog, who is clearly winning this race. He recommends obedience training, so we sign up for a class at a local school.

After taking him for a few weeks, it becomes apparent that he doesn't get the message. For Andy, this is an opportunity to mingle with other dogs. He has already won over two border collies, one Labrador retriever, and a very shy beagle. He is more of a community organizer than a trainee!

We are encouraged to purchase a "choke" collar before our next session and become comfortable using it to gain control of Andy, but we just can't seem to pull him that hard. Yanking him into submission is too cruel and not our style at all.

It's apparent to everyone else that Sir Andrew really has been training us all this time! We may not have received a certificate for completion of the course, However, more importantly, he loves children and remains a trusted guardian and companion for the son we would soon adopt for years to come.

The Way We Were

*O*n the outskirts of a small community near the Canadian border, our first home offers a sweeping view of the St. Lawrence River, a major navigation lane for commercial ships connecting the Great Lakes and Atlantic Ocean and home to the Seaway.

A backyard feeder sits high on our property and the binoculars are always at the ready for this "bird's eye" view where blue jays and brilliant red cardinals share the wealth with small chickadees, sparrows, and an abundance of bright yellow finches. A pileated woodpecker off in the distance is busy drumming and burrowing deep into crevices and holes, storing up winter food.

With night falling, the haunting sound of a foghorn announces the approach of a "Great Laker" far out at sea. Distant lights illuminate the ship's hull, serving as a beacon to warn other vessels away. We are hoping for just one more addition to complete us and make our house a home.

Six months after being approved for adoption, I receive

the phone call notifying us that a baby boy is now available. Leaving the workplace behind, my husband arrives home on a Friday evening, and I hurry outside as he parks the car. With his briefcase in hand and mandatory sport coat slung over his shoulder, he listens as I explain our good news.

That evening we call our families and the following morning drive home with our precious cargo. Our baby boy has been traveling for the first six weeks of his life to arrive in our town with a hunger for so much more than just food.

Hardly a natural at parenting, my excursions into babysitting have been short-lived, involving the supervision of older children already "potty" trained. Resembling a couple of ferrets, we are nervous and terribly alert!

Our first project involves mixing up a batch of formula in our new blender. Carefully reading the instructions, we turn on the blender and BAM! The lid flies off like a malevolent trajectory.

Our kitchen ceiling is spackled with formula and the sticky mixture slimes down our bathrobes and glasses. Hysterical laughter ensues as we finally release our pent-up emotions. Soon the sound of wailing fills the kitchen. Our baby is hungry and needs his bottle now—our young Pavarotti is making his presence known.

Our neighborhood is well established and composed of seniors with a host of grown children and grandchildren. Without much time to prepare, our supplies are few, but soon a bassinette, crib, playpen, and changing table appear on the scene from our generous North Country neighbors.

An impromptu baby shower hosted by my husband's coworkers provides us with many handmade items—all crocheted and knit with love in anticipation of a very welcome baby boy's arrival in our community. Their generosity and hospitality are a real blessing. Now prepared with everything we need, the one ingredient missing is experience.

Mom arrives on the scene with a trunk crammed with supplies. We dine on delicious stews and her famous roast beef sandwiches, ferried up to the North Country in the "Grandma Mobile." The three musketeers (Dad, Mom, and Grandma) hover around his crib, prepared for any emergency. If he startles awake or experiences discomfort, we are at the ready.

Seven hours later, our charge awakens after an uninterrupted night of rest to three sleep-deprived and groggy adults. An antique crib painted white will be our son's bed for quite some time. The room is painted a mellow yellow with light blue trim. Two framed needlepoints of Raggedy Ann and Andy, created by Aunt Sarah, grace the wall over the bureau. Our pantry is fully stocked for our first North Country winter.

Erma Bombeck provides my mother and I with some much-appreciated humor with stories from books entitled, *The Grass is Always Greener over the Septic Tank* and *At Wit's End*. Our evenings are spent reading her funny and poignant stories as our little one dozes off to the sound of laughter.

Chores are a labor of love for Mom. Whenever she arrives,

comfortable and matronly canvas shoes take the place of her high heels for security when carrying her grandson downstairs or out for a walk.

With her willingness to be involved in her grandson's life, my husband and I can have a weekend getaway, knowing that our son is in the best of hands. Living in the North Country for those first few years with our son is a precious memory and one of the happiest times for a grandma, a grandson, and two grateful parents.

Days of Wine and Roses

After five years in northern New York, my husband accepts a position in Human Resources in Syracuse. During this time, I begin to experience depression and my social drinking escalates. Alcohol begins to rob me of the maturity to live life on life's terms, and I remain in denial about how often and how much I am drinking.

While everything looks great on the surface, there is sadness and a hole in me that nothing and no one can fill—not even my beautiful son. Now back home, it is difficult to disguise my drinking and the obsession that accompanies it.

I am a "stay-at-home" mom in a community of predominately working-class families. Mom is still employed full-time and an aunt and uncle who live on the next street are both involved in the real estate business.

Our first winter there is challenging, given the amount of snow and cold temperatures, but eventually the snowy panorama entices us outdoors after being cocooned inside for weeks. First we bundle our toddler into his down snowsuit, then put on his boots and tie the fur-lined hood under his chin, as we head out the front door.

With his mittens on, he now resembles an adorable and wobbly baby penguin! As we traipse through the neighborhood with his hand in mine, we leave our footprints in the powdery snow.

The air is crisp and clean, and sounds are muffled. The hush is soon interrupted by the call of a cardinal perched on a barren branch in a small stand of trees. An elderly gentleman waves, quickly returning to the task of shoveling snow out of his driveway, before the next blitz of heavy snow descends. Arriving home, my son looks up at me with rosy cheeks and a mischievous "little boy" grin and my heart is full.

Nap time is quickly becoming a hassle for both of us. After climbing out of the crib following a twenty-minute catnap and the arrival of spring, I am faced with a dilemma. The idea of a small garden in our side yard is taking shape in my mind and provides us with a project.

My eager assistant, armed with a shovel and bucket, helps move stones and small rocks while a borrowed wheelbarrow transports larger rocks uphill to the empty lot behind our house. A trip to a local nursery provides us with fertilizer and young plants for our project.

With busy hands and his mind engaged, our young son is content to pull weeds and water the young plants. Soon our gardens are flowering in colorful profusion. Our family bond strengthens and the depression that dogs my every move seems to lessen.

When our toddler was out in the backyard, I used a wooden expandable gate to keep him where I could see him. During the summer months, Michael would have all his trucks and a small plastic wading pool with rubber boats and toys bobbing up and down, while Andy would circle the gate panting and looking for a cool place to plop down and rest.

One afternoon, I let my attention stray for just a few minutes. Returning to the kitchen window, I see Andy and Michael penned up together. It seems that our smart toddler simply lifted the gate and invited Andy in. This proved very amusing until, comes the dawn, when I realize that the gate is now totally useless. All it took was ten minutes with an active toddler and adoring guardian to turn everything upside down.

We make several trips to Pennsylvania to visit my husband's family, where our son is welcomed with open arms. My husband has two brothers still living at home and another brother living in Maryland. On our first visit, Grandma whisks her grandson away to meet the neighbors who have been waiting for his arrival. Grandpa holds him and tells him stories about the coal mines where he worked for so many years. Like many of the miners, he has been diagnosed with black lung disease and suffers greatly.

Suddenly our son has two new uncles who play with him constantly. After settling our son down for the night, I retreat to the kitchen where a large cabinet sits in the corner of the room. Having been encouraged to make myself at home, I fix myself the first of several stiff drinks and eventually land on the lumpy, familiar sofa where I fall asleep. At 3:00 am, the sound of heavy footsteps stumbling up the back stairs awakens me.

An alcohol-fueled testosterone turmoil ensues as three very inebriated men arrive on the scene. My husband and his two brothers return from the local hangout where the beer flows freely. Soon the only sound in the house is the intermittent snoring on the ocean of sleep. With one more for the road, I pass out on our double bed without turning down the covers or changing into night clothes.

The following morning, this "getting to know you" initial visit becomes awkward, with four of us gathered around the industrial-sized coffee pot sharing a king-sized hangover. Our little one takes center stage, while I silently pledge to abstain from liquor for Easter, even though my promise dissolves in a martini glass a few nights later.

With no thought of my father's struggle and the drink that held him captive, by 9:00 pm, I have already broken my sacrificial fast. Without knowing, my broken promises are building an impenetrable wall of shame around me.

A Moment of Truth

My first plump turkey is stuffed and placed in the oven. I unwind with a few shared drinks with my husband's family, who are spending the Thanksgiving weekend with us in our new home. Our son, Michael, is excited to spend time with his two bachelor uncles from Pennsylvania. They generously offered to help to prep and paint the outside of our three-bedroom ranch-style home in a suburb west of the city.

After a drive of three and one-half hours, everyone looks forward to a well-earned and plentiful dinner. Our pantry and bar are full, and the house has never looked so organized and clean.

My mind is focused on the future, with our home and shutters newly painted a barn red and window boxes filled with flowers. On an empty stomach and with a few strong cocktails, I am slightly buzzed and my attention to the meal wanes.

My mother-in-law returns from the kitchen and whispers to me "I don't think the oven is working." All the side dishes and vegetables are prepared and only need to be warmed in the oven, but I had neglected to turn on the oven hours ago! With a hungry toddler and a household of men working up a sizeable appetite, the chips and dips and cheese and cracker spread soon disappear.

In a panic, I turn to the phone book and call the Brooklyn Pickle nearby, hoping they are open and rushing there with just an hour to spare before they close.

With a spread of fresh submarine sandwiches and home-made soups on the kitchen table, I busy myself with making sure the dinner will go off without a hitch. Unfortunately, by the time dinner is ready to be served, I find all the men (including one toddler) sprawled out on the sofa and chairs in the living room, having exhausted their energy and succumbing to the dull, carbohydrate-propelled doldrums.

Forgiving and good natured, my in-laws enjoy the time spent with us. I am no longer in complete denial about my drinking, facing the fact that my drinking is beginning to take center stage in my life. The obsession and compulsion that accompany it prove relentless and I can no longer picture my life without a drink.

Fear ...
"Face Everything and Recover"

Employees are laid off due to downsizing and recent hires in management are let go. Our future is uncertain, and my husband is actively seeking employment locally, as well as out of state. After extensive interviewing, he accepts a position in Virginia.

With an offer on our house, I fly down to Virginia with my son and the three of us look for a new home. We rent a small two-story Cape Cod style home in the village. With my husband's thirty-minute commute to work, most of our adventures are on foot.

On Monday, we visit the grocery store, where our toddler pushes the cart down the aisles. On Wednesday, we visit the library for story hour, where I can see how much he enjoys being with children his own age.

Our son is enrolled in a local daycare program, where he can interact and socialize with other children his age. I return just in time to pick him up, having used the time to make phone calls and run a few errands.

Greeted with a cool reception, I quickly help him on with his boots and winter coat. Meanwhile, I am being admonished for failing to notify the staff that our son is not fully "potty trained."

Our son overhears the conversation, especially the part about not returning until he can stand in line with the other children and use the toilet without assistance. Both his father and I have spent time trying unsuccessfully to teach our son the art of being fully "continent," but he has informed us that he is just not ready yet. Bribery hasn't worked and even the fancy "big boy" wooden commode sitting alongside our full-sized toilet proves to be useless.

Just a few days after the episode at the daycare, our son manages to master the challenge and now wears his new superhero underwear. All it took was the right motivation for our strong-willed, determined son to announce, "I'm ready to go back to school!"

I receive an invitation to join a local business sorority and begin volunteering in our community. My first adventure is putting on puppet shows at the local library. The daycare brings the children on Mondays. After my son sits on the rug in the front, he proudly announces that the "Welcome Wagon" lady is his mom.

The sorority I joined holds a fashion show with proceeds going to a local charity. Looking out at the audience in the large auditorium, I have fortified myself with a few shots of brandy before the walk down the runway. I make it through the event without stumbling, but I can no longer predict or trust the outcome when drinking.

Singing, *Oh Shenandoah*, in the community chorus at a nearby junior college is a major accomplishment for me. The night of the concert, my husband and I arrive early. While he is seated in the audience, I sneak into the bathroom to fortify myself with some liquid courage out of a flask I carry in my purse.

Although there is no negative effect, it's the beginning of needing a drink even before I attempt to try something unfamiliar to me. Around this time, our social drinking enables me to host parties, and after moving into a larger home in a suburb, our popularity is on the rise.

On one occasion, several of our new neighbors are attending our first dinner party. Having spent the day preparing a lasagna, salad, and desserts, the idea occurs to me to have a relaxing drink before the guests arrive.

After my husband drops our son off at the babysitter's, we sit down to enjoy a few cocktails. While slipping into my silk dress and feeling a bit apprehensive, I fortify myself with a few more stiff drinks. While my husband showers, my martini slides down all too quickly. The doorbell rings and we're off to the races.

With the rug rolled up in the family room and speakers set up on our back deck, we are ready for dancing. The evening is a great success with appetizers and drinks flowing.

An hour after the last couple leaves, I return to the kitchen and open the refrigerator, only to discover the entire dinner. We had never brought out the food! We had all subsisted on appetizers and booze and no one seemed the wiser. We laugh it off, not wanting to see the unmanageability lurking just under the surface.

On her first trip to Virginia, my mother drives down with our large St. Bernard dog, Andy. Our veterinarian has provided medication to keep him comfortable for the long trip. This adds hours onto an already lengthy trip, since she stops at additional rest areas to walk Andy and make him comfortable.

Andy is like another member of the family to her, and she has always loved him despite his size. I can see how much responsibility my mother is assuming due to my lack of maturity. She arrives tired and yet so happy to be with us.

I realize what a position I have put her in, and another layer of guilt is forming. Fearful about my own ability to take charge of our household as a responsible adult, my social drinking is quickly becoming a necessity.

Mom makes the trip to Virginia from central New York during her vacation and on the holidays when she can. She usually arrives with a cardboard box containing several liquor bottles for our "parties" that we are holding with our neighbors and my husband's coworkers.

Planning to visit the state store later that day, I pour dry vermouth into a cup that morning. My young son walks by and grabs the Tupperware cup before I can reach him. He quickly pours some of the bitter liquid into his mouth, but immediately spits it out.

I can still see the expression on his face when he says, "Mommy, what is this awful stuff?"

It's the middle of that night when I wake up to find that I passed out again on the living room rug. I realize now that I was beginning to experience "blackouts," where I can't recall chunks of time leading up to the episode. My husband and son are asleep in their beds. I have no recollection of whether I kissed my son goodnight or thanked my husband for settling him in.

All I know is that somehow, I have crossed a line with my drinking. I can no longer imagine my life without a drink. Sobering up in a hospital on the psych floor was not my intention. I remember asking for help from our parish priest, because he comes and takes me there in the middle of the night.

The social worker visits me while I am an inpatient and asks me what I am going to do when I'm discharged. She provides me with a schedule of local AA meetings and encourages me to try.

Three days later, after being discharged, I attend my first AA meeting. It's just a few weeks before Christmas and without knowing, I am given the gift of desperation. God is doing for me what I cannot do for myself. We still manage to buy a real tree and decorate the house before my mother arrives for the holiday.

That Christmas would have been quite different, if it

weren't for those Wednesday and Saturday night meetings. As it was, I felt like I was walking around in a stupor, trying to find my way home.

After celebrating a year of sobriety with my group, I realize that I will need to make a change if I am to remain sober. Reality kicks in when I face my fears and say, "Okay, I was *nowhere* and through the grace of God I am *now here* and *now what?*"

Courage to Change

My husband agrees to an extended vacation for me and our young son. On a sunny morning in June, we load up the cars and I follow my mother back to my childhood home. There she welcomes us with open arms and a troubled heart.

What is meant to be an adventure escalates into a divorce that is difficult and painful, as I have no intention of returning. I also have kept this a secret from our son. My mother is aware of the impact this upheaval is having on her grandson, who misses his dad so much.

During the weeks that follow, I locate a meeting hall nearby and start attending AA meetings in the evening. With a part-time clerical position in a downtown bank, I'm traveling the familiar bus route from my childhood. I am gaining new acquaintances and I acquire some healthy self-esteem, based on my ability to learn and assimilate information.

What a relief to find that I haven't destroyed all the necessary brain cells from my drinking years. However, I remain in my own self-absorbed world, while my mother is the one providing the much-needed stability missing in my son's life.

Retiring early to take care of her grandson after school and on weekends, my mother's life is quickly filled with all the things required. Looking back, I realize she is the one who provides the much-needed stability missing from her grandson's life, while I am still caught up in my own self-absorbed world.

Finally, I receive a long overdue wake-up call when my mother takes me aside and tells me, "This is difficult and painful to say. While I always love you, there are times when I don't like you. Right now is one of those times."

This becomes a pivotal point for me in my sobriety, knowing that she loves me enough to tell me this for my sake and for my son's as well. One of the promises in our fellowship is, "Self-seeking will slip away." This requires living life on life's terms and having emotional sobriety.

While I have achieved physical sobriety, all of this is dependent upon my spiritual condition. Attending Big Book and Twelve and Twelve meetings, I become an active member of my home group.

My relationships are slowly being restored as I learn how to make amends and establish healthy boundaries for myself and with others. Where I have been emotionally unavailable to my son, I am now here as a sober mom, who can laugh with him and not take everything so seriously.

I still cling to some of my shortcomings, because they are

familiar to me. However, I know the easier, softer way, so if I keep it simple, one day at a time, I find balance in my life.

If I keep attending meetings and remain teachable, I have a good chance of remaining sober. With the help of my sponsor, I learn that I'm only as sick as the "secrets I keep." While I uncover, discover, and discard the ones that have kept me in bondage, there is much joy and freedom to walking in the sunlight of the spirit.

A New Freedom and a New Happiness

Standing at the podium and staring out at a sea of unfamiliar faces, I search for one man—the ghost of my father. He spent many of my early years in residence here at a facility for chronic and late-stage alcoholics. He died in the very town where we've come to share our experience, strength, and hope.

While traveling here with a group of recovering alcoholics like myself, I reflect on my father's helpless and hopeless state of mind and body that carried him toward a liquor store in the dead of night. He was found unconscious and died shortly after being discovered at the side of the road.

I share about the longing and loneliness for the father I have never known and the experience of growing up in a single-parent home with my mother and grandparents. Some of the men nod in agreement, as though identifying with the pain that I am experiencing here.

I share my journey through the Twelve Steps and the many

Big Book studies I have attended. I talk about my sponsor, my spiritual guide and mentor, who knows every detail of my last drunk and the many drinks preceding it. Remembering some of the slogans, I share how they have helped me.

Phrases like "Keep It Simple," "This Too Shall Pass," "Keep Coming Back," and "One Day at a Time" are often mentioned in meetings. When I heard, "We will love you until you can love yourself," I had serious doubts about trusting these words or a "Life beyond your wildest dreams." Laying out the tools of recovery as presented to me, I share my journey from "Nowhere" to "Now Here" to "Now What" and how my life has changed.

Finally, I refer to a sign on the clubhouse wall where I sobered up and attended meetings for the first few years in Alcoholics Anonymous. The sign reads, "YOU NEVER HAVE TO BE ALONE AGAIN." These comforting words offered me a way out of a hopeless, helpless state of mind and body.

"I was sitting in one of those chairs, with little hope for a sober future." These are words spoken by a man named Louie, who rode with us in the van. Louie explains how he came to believe in a power greater than himself and walked out of there a free man ... free of the bondage of self.

Louie remembers my father from the time he was committed here. Without the ability to admit defeat and surrender, my father suffered greatly. However, when AA was introduced to him as a solution, he just couldn't accept the powerlessness over alcohol or try what for many of us is the "easier, softer way."

I also understand for the first time that even cut off from me, my father loved me. The program promises that "we will know a new freedom and a new happiness" and "know how to handle situations that used to baffle us." I am an alcoholic like my father and his father before him. The only difference between us is that I chose the path of recovery.

A NEW NORMAL

*Taken by social worker on floor at Loretto with
mom (Sarah Jane) and I capturing Mom's
wonderful smile and my joy in being with her.*

Surprise trip to Mohonk Mountain House
to celebrate our Anniversary

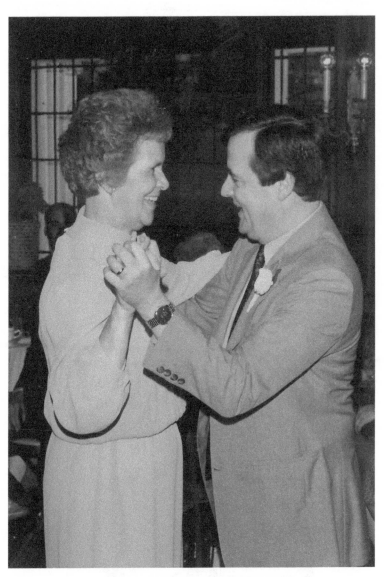

Mom and Ken (Her Son-In-Law)
dancing at our wedding 10/19/85

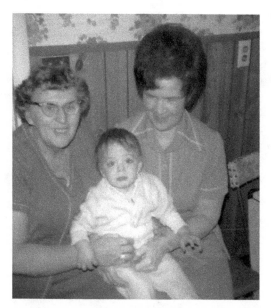

Tessie and Sarah Jane
Two proud grandmas with Michael (one-year-old)

Ken and I shortly after our
engagement is announced… crazy in love!

Gentle on My Mind

Just after 6:00 am on a Saturday morning, I awaken briefly to the sound of a car in our driveway. Thinking it might just be a car turning around, I drift back to sleep for a few more hours.

A beautifully wrapped arrangement of silk flowers in my favorite shades of blue and lavender is waiting on the porch step. Opening the card attached, I recognize my mother's handwriting.

Mom is struggling with her day-to-day functions and yet she can drive here and bring me this gift. The note printed with a shaky hand is signed, "To Patty from Mother. I am so proud of you." She has remembered this AA anniversary and what it represents. I cherish this moment.

My son and I still reside with Mom two years after arriving back in central New York. Michael and his dad are in communication on a regular basis and starting to spend more time together.

I agree to a "blind date" arranged by a girlfriend. My son and I drive over to her apartment to meet "Ken" and have dinner together. It was the first of many pleasant evenings. Finally, on New Year's Eve, Ken meets my mother for the first time, as we head out for an evening of dining and dancing.

Michael's grandmother is understandably skeptical and wary of this handsome stranger. Her grandson, Michael, is going through a tough time without his dad. My Irish mother proves to be quite the challenge.

A few months after we start dating, Ken leaves on a work-related trip to Florida, stopping off at Epcot before flying home. Arriving at her doorstep, he presents my mother with a basket of various hand soaps and floral bath salts purchased at a gift shop. My son has a new video game while I open an impressive box of Godiva chocolates.

Her comment after Ken leaves is priceless. My mother exclaims, "Doesn't he think I bathe?" Ken's sense of humor and honest, lighthearted spirit win her over. He becomes an activist for her care, determined and constantly supportive.

While employed at Catholic Charities, I overhear a conversation between two of my coworkers, parent aides in the Alliance program where I am employed as a secretary. One of the women also works part-time at a nearby nursing care facility.

At the mention of "Loretto" and "Sarah Jane," I realize they are discussing my mother. Even in that setting, she inspires others with her ability to accept her condition with as much dignity as the disease allows.

The serenity prayer that I recite at my meetings offers me the same hope and acceptance that were always a part of my mother's journey. I could not have asked for a more constant source of spirituality and love.

From "No Where" to "Now Here" to "Now What?"

U ncle Art escorts me down the aisle where Ken is waiting with a bright smile. He keeps pointing down at his shoes, but I'm too jittery to look.

After the wedding ceremony, while Ken sits in a pew putting on his dress socks, my Aunt Sarah questions him. He responds, "She knocked my socks off when I met her. I want her to remember that—always."

Without hesitation, my mother agrees to stay at our house with her favorite grandson. Michael looks forward to spending time with his grandmother, who drives him to his favorite bookstores in search of the latest Marvel comic books.

They leave early Saturday morning. With the train schedule in my mother's purse, they drive to the train station nearby to listen to the approaching locomotive's sound as it zooms into the station. Like two teenagers, they dine on takeout pizza and watch Michael's favorite movies, "Grandma approved for viewing."

Ken and I embark on a weekend trip to Greenwich, Connecticut, to attend a family wedding. We are confident about leaving Mom and her grandson together. However, during the wedding reception, we receive a call from a tearful and frightened son telling us that "Grandma is losing it." My mother has wandered away from the bench in the mall where she is guarding her grandson's comic book collection. Michael finally spots her looking into a store window, completely unaware of her surroundings. While driving them to the mall, my mother also became confused and runs a red light.

A few months later, my mother is diagnosed with Alzheimer's disease. Gone is the confident and proud banking executive. In her place stands an uncertain and vulnerable woman, looking out at the world through the eyes of a child.

Watching the light go out of her eyes is alarming for our family. There have been several near misses with charred pots on the stove and important papers scattered all over the table-top in no apparent order.

My mother has been an active participant in her church. As a Eucharistic Minister, she always arrives early for the service. However, one night she drives to the church after midnight and becomes alarmed to find the church doors locked, so she calls us.

Even though we reassure her, it is now becoming apparent that she can no longer live independently. While I am working, she is given an evaluation and told that she can no longer drive or manage her own household. Therefore, a decision needs to be made. How difficult will it be for her to lose the security and independence that her home provides?

Ken is a strong advocate for my mother. Although we are recently married and live in a three-bedroom starter home in Minoa, Ken is more than willing to bring his new mother-in-law to live with us.

Our lives change considerably over the next few months while establishing a routine. We struggle with Mom's inability to communicate her needs, while her young grandson also struggles with the loss of the special relationship he has always shared with her.

As the disease progresses, we realize that little is known about treatment or a possible cure. Juggling the role of being a mom to my young son is familiar to me, but often the role of being mom to my own mother seems impossible.

After attending a support group for Alzheimer's disease and with the guidance of professionals in the community, we enroll Mom in a day program for Alzheimer's patients. They shower her with love and pay personal attention to her needs.

The van picks her up every weekday morning and delivers her home in the late afternoon like clockwork. She becomes a part of a community where everyone works together to maintain a sense of self and where memories, music, and laughter are encouraged.

The 500-pound Canary

My husband always knows how to bring a smile to his mother-in-law's face. His sense of humor carries us through the most difficult and challenging of times. Ken prides himself in being able to tickle Mom's funny bone.

On the weekend, he insists on making her lunch and engaging her in the process. He develops creative ways to present her with her sandwich and gives her a clue to guess what it consists of. She often succeeds—a BLT (bacon, lettuce and tomato) and HST (ham, Swiss cheese, and turkey) on marbled rye bread are some of the favorites.

They have a running joke that always relieves any tension in our home. He asks, "Jane, what sound does a 500-pound canary make?" Eager to please, she responds with a loud "C … H… I… R… P," delivered in a deep, throaty voice I hardly recognize.

My husband knocks on the bathroom door. It seems that Mom is downstairs in the kitchen, and I am being instructed to look after her. Having just dressed Mom for her trip to the day program, I've taken a quick shower before heading off to work.

Grabbing my bathrobe, I hurry down the stairs. There in the morning light stands my mother staring at the clock on the kitchen stove. She is wearing a bright smile on her face and nothing more.

I step back and take a deep breath, remembering how my Irish grandfather, Thomas Francis Joseph Aloysius could diffuse almost any situation by using his Irish wit. I laugh my way through the frustration of bringing her back to her bedroom and hustle her back into her clothes while saying, "Nice try, Mom, but you can't greet the world in your birthday suit!"

Late one night, I awaken to my husband's whispering in the narrow hallway between our bedroom and my mother's. He isn't fond of pajamas so it's no surprise when he and my mother both open their bedroom doors at the same time, only to discover that they are both naked! My mother backs up and quietly closes her bedroom door. My husband is resolved to wearing his briefs after that.

My mother has always been modest and private with her hygiene—probably like me, as a result of her Irish Catholic upbringing. I hear her humming in the bathtub while I wait outside the door. She calls out to me, "Patty, I'm ready." The familiar scent of Ivory soap and Yardley talcum powder provide a healing balm, as I towel dry this little girl in a woman's body.

Bliss and Blisters

Ken is quick to comment on our relationship after being married for over twenty years. Reflecting on our marriage, I now see the value in the statement, "Marriage is a series of bliss and blisters."

Over the years we've been together, we've experienced physical and emotional pain and always came back stronger for it. I understand now that my peace of mind cannot be dependent on another person. The longer I remain in recovery, the more I mature.

We remained in our marriage, because we discovered the worth of hanging in there long enough to celebrate the blisters together and still experience bliss. We both changed over the years—Ken by becoming a more sensitive and vulnerable man, while I learned how to "toughen up" and develop a slightly thicker skin.

The pandemic changed our lives and taught us that every moment is precious. I have acquired enough strength to realize that our blisters led to a deeper and more meaningful relationship, and I am so grateful for the memories and moments of bliss that nothing can ever take away.

"When the student is ready, the teacher appears." My mother, Sarah Jane, became a valuable teacher. Our family was seated at a long table in a crowded restaurant on Thanksgiving.

While everyone was studying the menu and carrying on conversations, I looked up to see my mother trying to join in. Unable to communicate her sense of loss, her tears revealed the sadness in her heart.

There was no bliss involved in her journey that we could see—just painful blisters forming one after another. While we were there for her, she needed so much more than we could provide. Yet somehow, my mother found a way to remain present to us and her silent, stoic resignation became a surrender. Her faith was her strength and bliss.

My mother taught by example how to accept the unacceptable and live in the moment. She taught me the value in the statement, "Go and be no one." I try to arrive with no expectations or agenda, believing that I am enough, have enough, and do enough just the way I am, wearing the world like a "loose garment." For me, that's something worth holding onto.

She laughed with her son-in-law because he loved and admired her simply the way she was. His sense of humor lightened the weight of her illness for her and for me as well. Without even trying, he brought meaning and bliss into her life.

Amazing Grace

Now, finally, the final step in Mom's care arrives. The staff at the nursing home assure us that Mom will settle into a new routine. The social worker, Fran, offers us moral support and assures us that we are doing this for her safety and wellbeing. It does not feel like the right thing when she follows us back to the elevator, waiting to go home with us.

With the help of the nurses and aides, we make sure that her care is as complete and complementary to her personal needs as possible. Ken brings home a printout of the monthly menu to give his input into her diet and he becomes acquainted with the staff on her floor. Having been recently laid off from a management position, he is able to be there and meet all the people who interact daily with his mother-in-law.

On Sunday mornings, I accompany Mom in her wheelchair to the church service where she continues to amaze me by effortlessly reciting the Lord's Prayer and singing the words to *Amazing Grace* and *Let There Be Peace on Earth*.

We revisit the joys of simple pleasures. Mom comes home

for dinner and walks in the neighborhood. At Webster Pond, the squawking geese nibble at our fingertips as we feed them.

For pancakes covered with warm maple syrup, slathered with real butter and whipped cream, we go to Perkins. At a nearby popular summer haunt, we sit in the car, indulging in malted milk shakes. Mom's smile is infectious, as she delicately licks pistachio ice cream out of her sugar cone.

Many times, when I come to visit, Mom is in her room, sitting up in bed with a pillow tucked behind to support her back and gazing towards the window. Whether it's gloomy or a bright sunny day, it really doesn't matter—her smile is constant.

I pull the chair up to her bed and lean over. I softly ask my mother if she sees Jesus when she looks toward the window. My mother looks at me and nods her head up and down several times.

I choose to believe that she is seeing the presence of her faith, manifested there, the God she learned about, prayed to, and honored all her life. This remains for me a personal and private experience and a privilege to witness. The Serenity Prayer that I recite at my meetings offers me the same courage, hope, and acceptance that were always a part of her journey and, hopefully, will continue in mine.

Following a trial of antidepressants, I watch a listless and frightened lady grow strong again. She begins to eat what appears to be bland, tasteless food and enjoy it. She is again sitting up in her chair like a proud matronly queen and we have her back for a while.

Eventually the medication becomes less effective, and the drug will either need to be adjusted or discontinued. Given the nature of my mother's illness, the decision is made to remove the medication from her treatment plan.

There comes a time when a frail and spirit-broken Mom can no longer smile or respond to her name. She develops pneumonia and for a few weeks, it appears that this is the beginning of the end.

A few weeks before my mother passes, we receive a call during the night. Aspirating food becomes a problem and even ingesting pureed food can be difficult. Mom is having difficulty breathing and needs more than the staff can provide. The decision must be made whether to call for an ambulance or keep her comfortable.

Arriving at the hospital shortly after she has been admitted, the attending physician speaks to us prior to examining her. Having been oxygen-deprived for a period, we learn that her quality of life will not improve even with their intervention. My mother, a devout Catholic, would request Last Rites if she could, so very quickly a priest assigned to the chapel arrives to administer them.

Just fifteen minutes after the priest leaves, the physician approaches us. Her vital signs are dramatically improving, and the decision is made to put her in ICU and monitor her.

While it's unusual, I am allowed to bring Hospice in to facilitate her passing. A lay minister from a nearby Catholic

Church arrives. His name is David and together we pray for my mother.

Later, David approaches the desk, and my mother is administered a pill to prevent seizures. For three days, she remains in a state approaching death. While the supplemental oxygen is keeping her somewhat comfortable, the reality is that I will need to make the decision to have it removed, which could speed up her passing.

While sitting in the lounge, a female doctor approaches me. Tears are streaming down my face, and I just have no idea what to do. She helps me sort through my options. With my family and the hospice provider, I stand by the bedside and watch the final life support being removed.

Reflecting on the countless ways she has blessed my life and guided me through the rough patches, I celebrate her life thanking her for each memory of love and kindness and laughter she's shared with me.

I recite some of her favorite prayers. Her grandson arrives at the hospital and privately spends time with the grandmother who has always been there for him. Ken recognizes her for being a wonderful woman who presented him with many challenges while he was dating her daughter. Her heart softened dramatically on our wedding day when they shared a waltz on the dance floor.

Deciding to stay later that day, we take the elevator down to the cafeteria. Before leaving her room, I had turned around and said, "Mom, we're just going to the cafeteria for lunch, but we'll be back shortly."

A few minutes later, a nurse approaches our table with a somber expression on her face to inform us that Mom has passed. Whether it's by choice or God's timing, we can't be sure. It is enough to know in my heart that she was never alone, because she carried her trust and faith with her into each moment.

Her garments in the nursing home consisted of back snap dresses in busy floral prints and white athletic socks with her name printed on them. Imagine anyone wanting to steal those socks! She left this world quietly. However, while all signs of her physical presence are absent, her spirit remains, and we are blessed.

My mother has been gone for a while now. Pausing in the doorway of her small bedroom, I recall the precious time when she shared her "otherworldly self" with us; my mother/ my child.

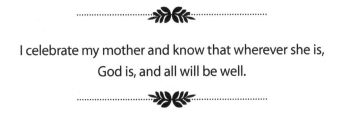

I celebrate my mother and know that wherever she is, God is, and all will be well.